Mahatma Gandhi

FATHER OF THE NATION

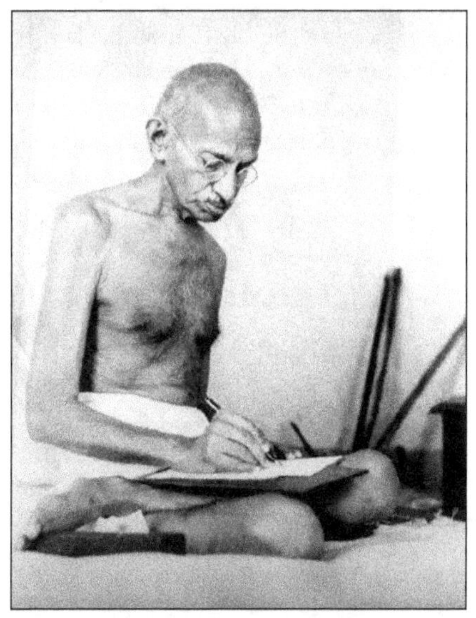

Manasvi Vohra

V&S PUBLISHERS

Published by:

V&S PUBLISHERS

F-2/16, Ansari Road, Daryaganj, New Delhi - 110002
☎ 23240026, 23240027 • *Fax:* 011-23240028
✉ info@vspublishers.com • 🌐 www.vspublishers.com

 **Online Brand Store: amazon.in/vspublishers**

Regional Office: Hyderabad
5-1-707/1, Brij Bhawan (Beside Central Bank of India Lane)
Bank Street, Koti, Hyderabad - 500 095
☎ 040-24737290
✉ vspublishershyd@gmail.com

Follow us on:   

BUY OUR BOOKS FROM: AMAZON   FLIPKART

© Copyright: *V&S* PUBLISHERS
ISBN 978-81-978303-2-7
New Edition

Publisher's Note

Since the beginning of our operations in 2010, **V&S Publishers** has been devoted to bringing you one of the best and widest selections of books from across reading genres. Our work is defined by our very name, Value and Substance (V&S), which is at the heart of the books we publish. In becoming one of the leading publishers of general trade books in the mass-appeal genre in India, we have focused on developing a repertoire of titles that not just seek to inspire our readers to grow and flourish in life, but also spark a love for varied cultures and languages. Today, our catalogue has expanded to more than 1000 titles, across the categories of academic, children's stories, parenting, popular science, religion and spirituality, self-improvement, and many more.

Mahatma Gandhi, the Father of the Nation, stands as one of the most revered figures in modern history. His principles of Satya (Truth) and Ahimsa (Non-Violence) along with his unwavering commitment to justice and equality have left an indelible mark on the world. This biography delves deep into his life and legacy, tracing his life journey from his early days in Porbandar, his experiences as a lawyer and activist in South Africa to his pivotal role in India's struggle for independence.

We hope that this biography will establish an understanding of his ideals, his strategies and their relevance in today's world while offering a comprehensive account of Gandhi's personal and political life and the profound impact he had on masses.

We sincerely hope our effort in bringing out this offering will be greeted by the warm and enthusiastic reception of our readers.

Contents

Childhood and Early Life

Mohandas Karamchand Gandhi was born on 2nd October 1869, in Porbandar, a princely state located in Kathiawad (Saurashtra) that is now part of Gujarat. He was born to Karamchand Uttamchand Gandhi and Putlibai in a Gujarati Hindu Modh *Baniya* family. Karamchand Gandhi came from a respected family in Porbandar and nearby areas, such as Rajkot and Junagarh. His ancestors belonged to the village of Kutiana in the then Junagadh State.

While his family was not known for their wealth or academic achievements, Karamchand Gandhi held the prestigious position of the "Dewan" or Chief Minister of Porbandar. Karamchand proved to be a capable chief minister despite having only completed his elementary school and having previously worked as a clerk in the state bureaucracy. He married four times while he was in office. His first two wives passed away when they were young, each having given birth to a daughter, and his third marriage produced no offspring.

A Blessed Birth
Mahatma Gandhi's birthday, 2nd October, is globally observed as International Day of Nonviolence.

*(a) Karamchand Gandhi: Father of
Mahatma Gandhi*

*(b) Pultibai Gandhi: Mother of
Mahatma Gandhi*

Karamchand requested his third wife's consent to remarry in 1857 and subsequently tied the knot with Putlibai that same year. Like him, she hailed from Junagadh and belonged to a Pranami Vaishnava family. Over the next 10 years, Karamchand and Putlibai had three children: Laxmidas, Raliatbehn, and Karsandas. Putlibai gave birth to Mohandas on 2nd October 1869, in the Gandhi family home in Porbandar.

Family Roots

Mahatma Gandhi's family was highly regarded for their honesty, wisdom, and their proficiency in administration and court matters. Their ability to handle citizens and situations with tact and loyalty was also well-known. Furthermore, their conduct in personal and public life was deeply respected by the people in Saurashtra. Irrespective of the situation, the members of the Gandhi family were known to act in difficult situations with courage and integrity. All this earned a highly respectable reputation of the Gandhi family across the region of Saurashtra.

According to history, the title of "Mahatma" was bestowed upon Gandhi by poet and Nobel Laureate Rabindranath Tagore. However, there is still a debate about it.

Rabindranath Tagore with M.K. Gandhi

Gandhi's grandfather, Uttamchand Gandhi, was a competent administrator who faced a predicament when he refused to comply with requests from the Queen Mother Regent's maids, leading to his falling out of favour with her. As a result, the Regent sent her army to his house, which was bombarded. Despite the attack, Uttamchand refused to back down and instead, decided to leave the Regent's service and move to Junagarh. In Junagarh, he went as far as to salute the Nawab with his left hand, which was a bold move!

When questioned about his gesture of disrespect towards the Nawab, he provided an explanation, stating that his right hand was committed to Porbandar. The Nawab was impressed by his answer and offered Uttamchand the position of the Dewan of Junagarh; which Uttamchand declined. This position was then offered to his son, Karamchand, who was appointed the Dewan at the young age of 24 years.

Uttamchand's son, Karamchand, was a highly principled individual, just like his father. During his tenure, he ran into troubled waters with the Ruler of Porbandar. Thereafter, he moved to Rajkot, where he was appointed the Dewan. During his time in Junagarh, Karamchand Gandhi ran into a conflict with the British authorities. He was displeased with the way the British political agent spoke about the ruler. As a result, he protested against the officer's behaviour. This led to his arrest and subsequent imprisonment. Despite this, Karamchand stood firm and refused to apologise for his actions. Eventually, the political agent was forced to withdraw his accusations and release him.

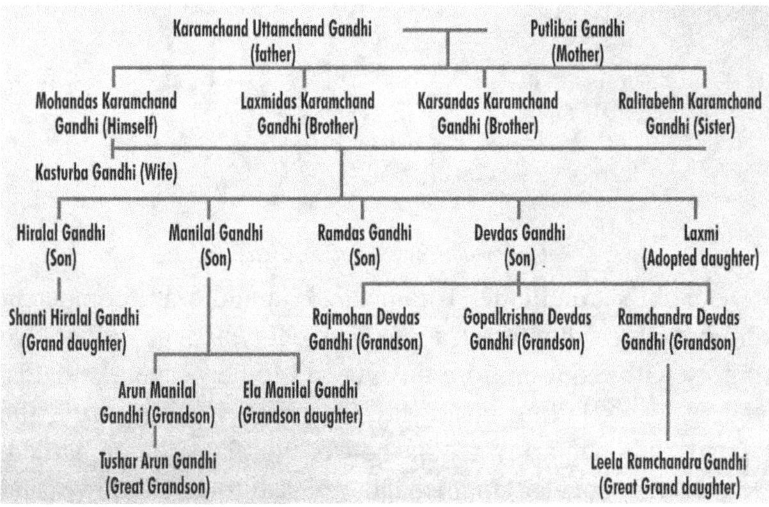

Family Tree of Mahatma Gandhi

Childhood Years

The Gandhi family had a diverse religious background. Mohandas's mother, Putlibai, came from a *Krishna bhakt pranami* tradition, which lent a lot of significance to religious texts, such as the *Bhagavad Gita*, the *Bhagavad Purana*, and 14 more texts describing the essence of the Vedas, the Quran, and the Bible.

Although Putlibai did not receive extensive education, she was a woman of intellect who could engage in discussions with women of the Royal family. Being devout Hindu, she would visit the temple regularly, keep fasts, and wouldn't eat her meals reciting her prayers. Although young Mohandas accompanied her to the temple, each day he did not much enjoy the pomp and show of the rituals. However, Mohandas was moved by his mother's unwavering devotion to God and her faith in religion.

<table>
<tr><td>Hard Vows</td></tr>
<tr><td>During the rainy season, Putlibai would make a promise to herself not to eat until she caught sight of the sun. Unfortunately, her vow often went unfulfilled because the sun would disappear behind the clouds by the time her children, who had noticed the sun's appearance, alerted her to come out and witness it for herself. As a result, she would go without food on numerous occasions.</td></tr>
</table>

Both Karamchand and Putlibai were very religious people. They would often invite religious leaders belonging to different faiths, including Jain, Muslim, and Parsi, to their house for religious discussions. The family would also listen to readings of the *Bhagavad Gita* and *Ramayana*. Young Mohandas grew up listening to these readings a sense of piety, devotion, and tolerance in his early years.

He was also deeply impacted by the stories about Raja Harishchandra, who dedicated his life in search of truth. The story of Harishchandra reinforced Gandhi's existing fascination with truth and his unwavering determination to uphold it, regardless of the cost to be paid. These virtues went on to form the foundation of his principle of religious tolerance in his adult life.

School Days and Marriage

When Mohandas Gandhi turned 9 years old, he started attending a local school in Rajkot. He studied history, geography, arithmetic, and Gujarati language in school. By the time he turned 11, he was moved to Alfred High School in Rajkot. In school, Mohandas was shy but a diligent student. Although he wasn't much into sports, but he won many prizes for his outstanding performance in sports. He didn't have many friends in school hence, as soon as school would get over, he would run back home.

A Football Fan

Although Gandhi was not into sports when he was in school, he grew up to become a huge fan of the game of football. He even formed two football clubs, one in Pretoria and another in Johannesburg, in South Africa.

In May 1883, when Mohandas was 13 years old, he entered an arranged marriage with Kasturbai Makhanji Kapadia, who was 14 years old at the time. Consequently, he had to forego a year of his schooling. However, he was later offered the opportunity to make up for the lost year by accelerating his studies. The wedding was a shared event, where his brother and cousin were also married. Kasturbai – who was later known as Kasturba – spent much of her time at her parents' place as she was an adolescent then.

Mahatma Gandhi with his wife Kasturba Gandhi

2

Education and Early Years as an Activist

Tragically, in 1885, when Mohandas was only 16 years old, his father, Karamchand, passed away. This event deeply impacted young Gandhi who had also just lived through the death of his first child. Two consecutive deaths had left Gandhi deeply anguished. In the following years, Gandhi and Kasturba had four children: Harilal who was born in 1888; Manilal in 1892; Ramdas in 1897; and Devdas in 1900.

After his father's death, Gandhi found himself at crossroads about the way forward. He completed his high school education in 1887. But since there was no college in Rajkot then, had to move to Samaldas College in Bhavnagar. However, studies proved to be difficult here as all the subjects were taught in English and Gandhi's knowledge of the language was limited then. Soon, he dropped out of college and returned to his family in Porbandar.

Kasturba Gandhi with her children

Off to London

At this point Gandhi was faced with a choice: he could head to Bombay to continue his studies or stay in his hometown and look forward to serve as the Dewan, as was tradition in their family. But neither of these ideas appealed to him. And this was the moment when he thought about moving to England to qualify for the Bar – it would not just award him a prestigious qualification, but also offer a way to rub shoulders with the elite.

<table>
<tr><td align="center">The Three Vows</td></tr>
<tr><td>Obtaining his mother's consent for moving to England proved to be a challenging task. After much coaxing by friends and family members, Gandhi's mother finally relented. She agreed to let him go on the condition that he make three solemn vows: to abstain from meat, wine, and women. Gandhi accepted these conditions and proceeded to Bombay enroute to England.</td></tr>
</table>

In Bombay, Gandhi was countered by the elders of the cast who implored him not to move to England, with threats that he and his family will lose favour in the community. However, At the time all of 18, Gandhi stood his ground and told them that while he respected them, he was not going to change his mind. Years later, Gandhi remarked this as his first stint with *satyagraha* even though he did not fully understand the essence of this act at that time.

On 4th September 1888, Gandhi embarked on a journey to England. Gandhi was aware of the significant challenges and opportunities ahead of him. To document his experiences, he started keeping a diary where he recorded his observations, feelings, thoughts, actions, and learning. He did not experience sea-sickness and was able to brave rough seas until he reached England.

In England, Gandhi started attending University College, in London. Initially, he found it difficult as his knowledge of English language was limited. Soon, he enrolled for classes in English literature. This was also when he joined Inner Temple since he wanted to become a barrister. After moving to London, Gandhi tried to overcome his shyness by participating in a public speaking practice group, which allowed him to pursue a career in law.

Vegetarianism in England

In England, Gandhi encountered new challenges with regards to his vegetarianism. He found it difficult to find vegetarian food and often had to subsist on a diet of bread and butter. However, Gandhi refused to compromise his principles and continued to abstain from meat and other animal products.

Gandhi and Vegetarianism

In addition to abstaining from meat, Gandhi also went on to practice dietary restrictions, such as fasting and abstaining from milk and dairy products, as a form of self-discipline and continued such practices for spiritual purification, later in life.

Thereafter, he began to look for restaurants in London that would serve vegetarian food. He finally came across one on Farringdon Street. At this restaurant, he came across the book, *Plea for Vegetarianism* by Henry Salt, which would go on to play a pivotal role in his life. The book's arguments in favour of vegetarianism reinforced his belief in following a vegetarian diet and how such a diet helped in maintaining a balance in one's body and mind. This was also when he learnt that there was a crucial difference between eating to nourish one's health and pleasing one's palate.

Gandhi joined Vegetarian Society and was soon elected into its executive committee. At the time, the president of the society was Arnold Hills. At the Vegetarian Society, Mahatma Gandhi met many members of the Theosophical Society – including Dr. Annie Besant and Madam Blavatsky. His experience at the Vegetarian Society was important, for it led him to gain a deeper understanding of the running, functioning, and management of institutions and such societies.

The Theosophical Society was devoted to the study of Buddhist and Hindu centric literature. Members of this society approached Gandhi to help them with the translation of the *Bhagavad Gita*. This led Gandhi to discover Edwin Arnold's English translation of the *Bhagavad Gita*, titled *The Song Celestial*. The depiction of the man of abiding wisdom deeply influenced Gandhi's thoughts, and the verses remained in his mind. He also read Arnold's *The Light of Asia* which described the life and message of the Buddha. Gandhi became engrossed in the book and was particularly struck by the Buddha's philosophy of renunciation and compassion, leaving a lasting impression on him.

Joining the Bar

In the middle of all his pursuits, Gandhi utilised his time to prepare for the Matriculation Examination of the University and to fulfill the requirements to qualify for the Bar. To achieve this, he studied Latin and read relevant books on Law. His efforts paid off as he passed his examinations and was called to the Bar on 10th June, 1891. Subsequently, on 11th June, he enrolled in the High Court before departing for India on 12th June.

However, upon landing in India, Gandhi was left shaken when he learned that his mother had died while he was in England. His family had not told him about it, thinking it would affect his studies and subsequent performance in examinations. Trouble followed upon his return to India as Gandhi couldn't set up his law practice in Rajkot. He wasn't familiar with Indian laws and faced competition from the locals.

He moved to Bombay and was finally able to get a client that led him to present his case in the Small Causes Court. But when it was time for cross-examination, he was unable to speak. All the events left his feeling worried about the future – how would he look after his family or repay his brother for the monetary assistance he had provided in sending him to England?

Initial Years of Activism in South Africa

Unexpectedly, a Muslim company in Kathiawar, which had an established business in South Africa, offered him a position. The company was involved in a legal dispute with another Indian

Muslim firm and sought Gandhi's assistance as their Chief Counsel. The terms of the offer were appealing, prompting Gandhi to accept and embark on a journey to South Africa to practice law and make money.

Upon his arrival in Durban in May 1893, he was greeted by Abdullah Seth, the head of the firm. However, Gandhi had no idea what lay ahead for him in this unfamiliar continent, and he soon realised that he would face some of the most challenging experiences of his life. As soon as he arrived in South Africa, Gandhi encountered discrimination based on his skin colour and heritage, which was a common experience for people of colour. The prejudice that he personally experienced and witnessed towards Indians from British people troubled him. This led him to question the standing of his people within the British Empire.

<table><tr><td>

Discrimination in South Africa

Gandhi faced severe discrimination in South Africa. He was denied place to sit with European passengers on a stagecoach and was instead instructed to sit on the floor close to the driver. When he refused, he was physically assaulted. Additionally, he was thrown off a train at Pietermaritzburg for declining to vacate the first-class section. However, he chose to advocate for himself and was eventually permitted to board the train the following day.

</td></tr></table>

Meanwhile, after the Abdullah case ended in May 1984, a farewell party was arranged by the Indian community in South Africa for Gandhi to see him off as he prepared to return to India. However, as fate would have it, Gandhi stumbled upon a copy of *Natal Mercury*. It carried an article regarding a forthcoming Bill that would deprive all Indians residing in Natal of their voting rights. Gandhi cautioned that if the Bill were to pass and Indians were to accept it, they would essentially be contributing to their own downfall. People were worried and hoped to resist the Bill, but it was unclear who should spearhead the effort.

As a result, Gandhi extended his stay in South Africa and decided to help the Indians to oppose the bill. A petition, which later signed by 500 Indians, was drafted by him to the Legislature. When it failed to be addressed by the Legislature, he wrote another petition to the Secretary of State for Colonies in Britain. It was met with support and garnered 10,000 signatures. This is how Gandhi began the task of opinion building among the public in South Africa and England.

Even though his efforts were ultimately unsuccessful in stopping the passage of the bill, it brought to light the deplorable condition of Indians in South Africa. In 1894, he founded the Natal Indian Congress which helped in bringing together Indians in South Africa into a solid political force. He would write articles in journals, petitions, and memorials, as well as organise meetings in the Indian community. During this time, he lived on meagre resources as he refused any compensation for public work. He only accepted fees for his legal counsel and later joined the Law Society as an advocate.

Tolstoy Farm was established by Mahatma Gandhi in Transvaal, South Africa

3

Activism in South Africa and Return to India

In the years that followed, Gandhi continued to fight against discrimination in South Africa. After taking leave for six months, he decided to return to India to bring his family to South Africa. He also aimed to raise awareness among the people and leaders in India about the mistreatment of Indians in South Africa and the harsh working conditions that Indian labourers faced in the country.

He travelled to various cities, including Bombay, Calcutta, and Madras. While in Bombay, Poona, and later in Madras, he had the opportunity to meet prominent leaders of that time. Some of the people who expressed their support for him included Lokmanya Bal Gangadhar Tilak, Gopal Krishna Gokhale, and Sir Pheroze Shah Mehta, among others. However, his visit to Calcutta was interrupted due to an urgent call from his colleagues in South Africa.

Upon receiving the summons, Gandhi decided to end his trip in India and head back to South Africa with his family in 1897. They travelled aboard the SS *Courland*, which belonged to Dada Abdullah, along with the *Naderi*. The latter ship carried 800 indentured labourers. However, upon arrival at the port, the ships were not permitted to dock due to the white population's anger. They had been incensed by a news report that Gandhi had distributed a malicious pamphlet against the whites of South Africa and was bringing numerous Indian labourers to flood the country.

In 2007, the United Nations designated Mahatma Gandhi's birthday, the 2nd of October, as the International Day of Nonviolence.

After being held off from docking for 23 days, the passengers of the ship finally deboarded on 13th May. Gandhi's family was sent to safety with Parsi Rustomji. However, Mr. Escombe, the Attorney General, sent him a message about the fiery mood of the whites and suggested to wait until nightfall to step out of the ship. At night, Gandhi stepped out of the ship, with Laughton, who was the legal advisor of Dada, Abdullah & Co., to reach Rustomji's house. However, just as they stepped out, they were surrounded by an angry mob that began to rain punches and blows on Gandhi. He was badly injured in the brawl, but was rescued in time by the wife of the Police Superintendent.

This incident elicited widespread remorse and sadness among people, even as far as London and other parts of the world. The Government of South Africa was requested by the Secretary of State for Colonies to locate and penalise those responsible. Gandhi was informed of these instructions by the Police Superintendent, who requested his assistance in identifying and punishing the culprits. Despite this, Gandhi harboured no resentment and informed the Government that he did not wish for any of his attackers to be prosecuted. A strong believer of *Dharma*, Gandhi did not believe in retaliation nor was there any bitterness in him against his attackers.

Fighting for Change in South Africa

As Gandhi was settling in with his family in Johannesburg and working to strengthen the Natal Indian Congress, which was fighting for the rights of the Indian community, other events were unfolding in South Africa. Notable among these was the period of the Boer War (1899–1902), which was fought between the British Empire and the Boer Republics over the former's growing control over South Africa.

In 1900, during the Boer War, Gandhi formed the Natal Indian Ambulance Corps with the intention of disproving British Colonial stereotypes about Indians' limited abilities in handling "manly" activities. He recruited 1,100 Indian volunteers who were trained and certified to serve on the front lines. They supported British troops in the war against the Boers. During the Battle of Spion Kop, Gandhi and his corps carried wounded soldiers over rough terrain for miles to a field hospital. For their services, Gandhi and 37 other Indians were awarded the Queen's South Africa Medal.

With time, Gandhi's activism in South Africa extended to raise awareness about the racial persecution of the Africans, besides Indians. He earned the appreciation of Nobel Prize winner, Nelson Mandela, for his relentless efforts to create a synergy between Indians and non-white South Africans against Apartheid.

The Indian Opinion

Mahatma Gandhi founded a newspaper, named *Indian Opinion*, in 1903, which became an important voice for the rights of Indians, as well as for political activism in South Africa.

However, a huge shift occurred in Gandhi's consciousness after the Bambatha Rebellion, in 1906, which took place in Natal. He swung into action, forming a volunteer-led stretcher-bearer unit, which consisted of both Indian and African stretcher-bearers to carry those wounded in the rebellion. Even after suppressing the rebellion, the Colonial administration refused to give the same civil rights to Indians as given to the white South Africans. This led to him awaken spiritually and become completed disillusioned with the Empire and the West, in general.

Standing for a Cause
Mahatma Gandhi organised several successful campaigns against discriminatory laws and practices, notably the Asiatic Registration Act.

In 1910, his newspaper, *Indian Opinion*, started covering instances of racial discrimination faced by Africans. Meanwhile, Gandhi was working on his methods of nonviolent protest as well. He established an idealistic community at Tolstoy Farm in Johannesburg, with the help of Hermann Kallenbach. In the following years, non-white South Africans were finally given the Right to vote and Gandhi was hailed as a national hero.

Copy of the certificate used to register Asian Men with their thumb impression

Gandhi's Return to India

Gandhi and his family left South Africa to return to India in July 1914. By now, Gandhi had established his reputation as a leading Indian theorist, community organiser, and a passionate nationalist. He arrived in Bombay and was given a huge welcome by Gopal Krishna Gokhale himself, who personally received him at the dock. One of the key leaders of the Congress Party, Gokhale was the force behind Gandhi at this point. He even introduced Gandhi to the issues and politics of prevailing in India back then.

During this time, Gandhi also had a landmark meeting with the great polymath, Rabindranath Tagore, who had set up Shantiniketan, in Bolpur, in West Bengal. Gandhi visited Shantiniketan, which was Tagore's centre of *sadhana*, and decided that it would serve as an ideal home, albeit temporarily, for his colleagues from Tolstoy Farm and Phoenix Settlement back in South Africa. Both had great respect for each other. During this visit, Gandhi received the sad news of Gokhale having passed away.

Gopal Krishna Gokhale was believed to be the Political Guru of Mahatma Gandhi

The Nobel Peace Prize

Mahatma Gandhi earned five nominations for the Nobel Peace Prize, but he never won.

In 1920, Gandhi took over the leadership of the Congress. He also set up his *ashram* at Kochrab, in Ahmedabad – the province where his hometown was located. This was followed by the setting up of an *ashram* along the banks of the Sabarmati river. In these years, Gandhi came to an understanding about truth in the form of *satyagraha*, which meant living a life which was based on the principle of truth. He believed that in both, personal and social life, one's actions should solely be based on truth. The *ashram* was seen as a spiritual community of activists. Those interested in joining the *ashram* had to take 11 vows to become a member.

(a) Kochrab Ashram was the first ashram established by Mahatma Gandhi in India

(b):Entrance of Sabarmati Ashram, started by Mahatma Gandhi

The Champaran Agitation

The first significant milestone that Gandhi achieved in India's struggle for independence was with the Champaran agitation. Gandhi was to attend a session of the Indian National Congress, in Calcutta. Here, he met a young man, named Rajkumar Shukla, who had come to see him from Champaran, in Bihar. Shukla made a representation of the problems faced by the peasants in Champaran owing to their exploitation at the hands of the British Colonial officials.

The British Colonial government had given special concessions to European planters in Bihar, which allowed them to exploit and oppress the local peasants. One such concession was the *Tinkathia* system, which required farmers to cultivate indigo on a third of their land and surrender the entire indigo crop to the British planters at a fixed price. The peasants were forced to grow indigo despite the crop's declining demand and the low price they received for it. They were also forced to work as indentured laborers on the plantations.

In 1917, Gandhi arrived in Champaran and investigated the situation. He met with the local farmers and educated them on their rights. He then launched a campaign of nonviolent resistance against the British administration. The British authorities arrested Gandhi, but it only led to more protests. Other Indian leaders also joined him in support of the peasants. Finally, the British government relented and the Champaran Agrarian Bill was passed in 1917. It provided relief to the farmers and abolished the oppressive *Tinkathia* system.

Postal stamp released by Government of India in 2017 to mark 100 years of Champaran Satyagraha

4

The Struggle for India's Independence

Mahatma Gandhi is considered the father of the Indian Independence Movement, which he led from 1918 until India gained independence in 1947. During these years, Gandhi pioneered numerous nonviolent and peaceful methods of resistance that are now collectively known as *satyagraha*.

After the success of Champaran agitation, Gandhi was chosen as the President of the Gujarat Sabha. Soon, he learnt about the condition of the peasants in the district of Kheda, in Gujarat.

Kheda Agitation Begins

Due to one of the most severe famines in 1918, Kheda had suffered crop failures, yet the government was insistent on the full payment of land revenue. Gandhi understood the peasants' cause to be fair and just. He told the peasants that they should be ready to engage in nonviolent resistance.

As a result, Gandhi encouraged them to withhold the payment of land revenue unless it was reassessed in view of the crop failures. If the government were to respond by seizing their property, farms, and bullocks, the peasants were instructed not to surrender or resort to violence.

A child once approached Gandhi and asked him why he was not wearing a shirt. Gandhi stated that he could not afford one. But the child suggested that his mother could make one for him. Gandhi, on the other hand, refused, claiming that he had a large family of 400 million brothers and sisters and that he could not wear a shirt until everyone else had one.

Gandhi relocated his base of operations to Nadiad and mobilised numerous followers and new recruits from the area. Among the most prominent connections he made at this point was with Sardar Vallabhbhai Patel, who was a barrister practising in Ahmedabad. Vallabhbhai went on to work with Gandhi as his colleague in all his endeavours throughout his life.

Mahatma Gandhi with Sardar VallabhBhai Patel

Employing non-cooperation as a strategy, Gandhi launched a signature drive in which farmers committed to refuse payment of revenue taxes even in the face of the seizure of their land. Although the administration was initially unyielding for a period of five months, by late May 1918, the Government relented on key provisions and eased the conditions for paying revenue taxes until the famine subsided. In both the case of Champaran and Kheda agitations, Gandhi had demonstrated *satyagraha* to be an effective way of protesting unfair laws and provisions and seeking justice.

Inception of Civil Disobedience Movement

With the end of World War I in 1918, the Indian National Congress (INC) held high hopes for greater freedom for India, and Gandhi was at the forefront of this movement. He believed in the British government's sense of justice and fairness and expected them to meet the Indian people's aspirations. However, the British government's response to the demands of the Indian National Congress was disappointing. Instead of granting greater freedom and self-government, they introduced the Rowlatt Bill in 1919, which proposed severe restrictions on the civil liberties of the Indian people.

Gandhi saw the Rowlatt Bill as a complete violation of human rights. He believed that the bill would give the government too much power and would lead to the suppression of Indians. As the leader of the INC, Gandhi called for a nationwide protest against the bill. This protest eventually led to the Jallianwala Bagh Massacre, in which hundreds of innocent civilians were killed. This tragic event was a turning point in Gandhi's life and marked the beginning of his nonviolent civil disobedience movement.

During this time, Gandhi spearheaded the Khilafat Movement. The movement aimed to protect the Ottoman Empire's caliphate, which was threatened by the British after World War I. In Gandhi's opinion, it was necessary to foster cooperation between Hindus and Muslims to achieve political justice. He believed that the issue of the caliphate was a matter of great importance to Indian Muslims and that it could serve as a catalyst to bring about Hindu-Muslim unity. The Khilafat Committee as well as the INC accepted the non-cooperation agenda. Gandhi was requested to spearhead the movement.

The movement sought to withhold cooperation from the government by boycotting various institutions such as schools, colleges, and courts of law. This led students to leave educational institutions, while prominent lawyers, including Motilal Nehru and C.R. Das, abandoned their practice. People were also encouraged to avoid seeking justice from government courts, and those who had been awarded titles and honours by the government returned them.

<table>
<tr><td>The Pen is Mightier than the Sword</td></tr>
<tr><td>Gandhi launched three weekly publications — Young India in English, Navajivan in Hindi, and Navajivan in Gujarati — to promote satyagraha and non-cooperation as well as to describe his idea of Swaraj (self-rule) and the individual and social efforts required for it.</td></tr>
</table>

Numerous national educational institutions were established in various locations to offer education to those who participated in the boycott of government schools. During this time, Gandhi himself founded the Gujarat Vidyapeeth. People's courts were established to resolve conflicts and bonfires were set up to burn foreign goods as part of his *Swadeshi* policy. Additionally, Gandhi asked Indians to set aside time every day to spin *khadi* as part of the independence movement.

The Intervening Years

The idea of non-cooperation became very popular among the Indian masses. However, Mahatma Gandhi decided to roll back the Noncooperation movement after violence erupted at Chauri Chaura in Uttar Pradesh. He believed that the masses were not fully ready to practice Satyagraha. Subsequently, Gandhi was arrested on 10th March, in 1922, and sent to Yervada prison, near Poona, for six years for speaking out against the government. While he was in jail, the INC split into two groups: called as Pro-changers one group – led by Motilal Nehru and Chittaranjan Das – wanted to participate in government, while the other group: called as No-changers – led by Sardar Vallabhbhai Patel and C. Rajagopalachari – did not want to be a part of the government.

The Khilafat Movement, which had brought Hindus and Muslims together, ended because of changes in Turkey. Muslim leaders left the Congress and formed their own groups. Gandhi's followers were no longer united. Gandhi was released from the prison after two years, in February 1924, because he needed to be operated for appendicitis. He was admitted to Sassoon Hospital in Poona.

In the intervening years after his release from Yervada prison, Gandhi devoted himself to the cause of fighting for *Swaraj*. The British government asked Indian leaders to create a proposal for constitutional reform that everyone agreed on. Motilal Nehru led a committee that made a set of proposals in response.

However, some of the younger leaders, such as Jawaharlal Nehru and Netaji Subhash Chandra Bose, were not happy with the idea of "Dominion Status" and wanted complete independence. At the Calcutta Congress in December 1928, Gandhi proposed a compromise. The Nehru Report would be accepted, but with a condition that if the British government did not grant Dominion Status within a year, the Congress would aim for complete independence and use nonviolent, non-cooperation to achieve it.

In 1936, Gandhi devised a diet for his political rival, Netaji Subhash Chandra Bose. The plan recommended eating more leafy vegetables and less starchy foods, as well as raw garlic and onion for their health benefits. Gandhi also advocated for the inclusion of dates and raisins in the diet, while claiming that tea and coffee were not required for good health.

Mahatma Gandhi and Subhas Chandra Bose

In Lahore, an Indian flag was raised on 31st December 1929. Congress, under the leadership of Gandhi, observed India's Independence Day on 26th January 1930 in Lahore.

Gandhi and the Salt Satyagraha

Gandhi issued a letter to Lord Irwin, the British Viceroy of India, in 1930, outlining his demands for the Indian people. One of these demands was the ability to produce their own salt, basic a necessity. The British government had imposed a high tax on salt, making it extremely expensive for the general public to purchase.

Lord Irwin rejected Gandhi's demands, leading to the Salt Satyagraha on 12th March, 1930. Gandhi and his followers marched to Gujarat's coast, where they began producing salt by evaporating seawater. In response, the British government arrested Gandhi and thousands of his followers. This sparked widespread protests and demonstrations throughout the country. The British government retaliated violently, and many Indians were beaten and imprisoned as a result.

Despite the violence, the Salt Satyagraha lasted nearly a year. It demonstrated that the Indian people had all the tools they needed to resist British rule peacefully and to make sacrifices for their freedom.

Gandhi and Lord Irwin reached the Gandhi-Irwin Pact in 1931, which resulted in the release of political prisoners and paved the way for future negotiations towards Indian independence. The Salt Satyagraha is still remembered as one of the most iconic events in Indian independence history.

Mahatma Gandhi at Tower Buiding during Dandi March

5

The Final Road to Victory

The Gandhi-Irwin Pact of 1931 marked a significant moment in the life of Mahatma Gandhi. The Pact was signed following a series of negotiations. Its main features included the release of political prisoners, the suspension of the civil disobedience movement, and the participation of the Indian National Congress in the Round Table Conference. However, Gandhi's decision to sign the Pact was met with opposition from some members of Congress. Similarly, there were British Officers who were at odds with Lord Irwin's efforts to strike a compromise.

The Congress did not attend the First Round Table Conference as there was no agreement on who should attend as a representative. The British government planned a second Round Table Conference to discuss further constitutional reform with Indian leaders. Despite objections to the process of selecting participants, the Congress decided to attend with Gandhi as their sole representative. However, the heavy responsibility of being the only representative for the Congress, combined with differences within the party, made Gandhi's task challenging.

The Round Table Conferences

During the Conference, Gandhi understood that the British had the strategy to depict the Indians as divided, pursuing conflicting interests, and therefore incapable of self-governance. The British propagated the notion that their presence was necessary to hold the country together and protect all interests, and the transfer of power was not feasible. Among the British officials, some openly expressed their opinion that Indians were not capable of self-rule. The government also manipulated the selection of attendees to create a stalemate.

Glimpses of Mahatma Gandhi attending the Second Round Table Conference

Meeting the King Emperor

The King-Emperor of England invited Gandhi to a "Tea Party" attended by delegates. Officials urged Gandhi to wear a three-piece suit to the event. However, Gandhi declined, stating that he represented India's poor and could not wear anything more than they would. Thus, Gandhi met the King while wearing only a loin cloth and shawl.

The British proposed a constitutional reform plan modelled after British Dominion, which included separate electorates based on religion and social class. They questioned the Congress Party's and Gandhi's authority to speak for all of India. There were also other Indian leaders, such as B.R. Ambedkar, Srinivasan Sastry, and Akbar Hydari, present at the place. Gandhi, on the other hand, was opposed to a constitution that legitimised communal rights or representation. He believed it would cause divisions among people and divert attention away from the goal of ending Colonial rule in India.

However, the Conference never arrived at any conclusion. Gandhi opposed the ideas of the British and clearly laid down the objectives of India as a nation. He relayed that there was no conflict of interests in India and that the British in fact had sown seeds of discord to create differences in order to deny the nation its freedom. He emphasised that any ideas or claims that were against the interest of the poor will need to be annulled in independent India.

Negotiations Within the Congress Party

Gandhi arrived in Bombay on 28th December, 1931, and openly admitted that he had not met his goal. He did not believe Britain would grant independence without a fight. Meanwhile, Willingdon, Irwin's successor, had undone the Gandhi-Irwin Pact's gains. Many Congress leaders had been arrested. Willingdon had imposed new restrictions on freedom, with thousands of people being imprisoned. The Congress Working Committee determined that the only option left was to resurrect civil disobedience.

In just one week after returning from London, Gandhi and the members of the Working Committee were taken into custody on January 4th. They were imprisoned at Yervada prison, along with his Secretary, Mahadev Desai, and Sardar Vallabhbhai Patel. During his confinement, the British government enacted the Communal Award, which granted untouchables a separate electorate. In response, Gandhi began a fast-unto-death, causing public outrage. The British eventually replaced the Communal Award with the Poona Pact, which was a compromise that was worked out after consultations with Dr. B.R. Ambedkar.

> In September 1932, Mahatma Gandhi and Dr. B.R. Ambedkar signed a pact called as the Poona Pact which ensured reservation for the Depressed Classes (Dalits) in electoral constituencies.

In 1934, there came a turning point when Gandhi resigned from the Congress party. However, in 1936, Gandhi made a return to politics, with the Congress convening the Lucknow session. Gandhi believed that the Congress should concentrate solely on achieving independence rather than speculating about India's future. But he did not prevent the party from adopting socialism as its goal.

In 1938, Subhash Chandra Bose was elected as the president of Congress for a second term, but ran into conflict with Gandhi over his disagreement with using nonviolence as a way of protest. However, Bose left the party when the All-India Congress leaders resigned in protest of his rejection of Gandhi's principles.

The Landmark Quit India Movement

When World War II broke out in 1939 India was still a British colony. The British government desired India's participation in the war effort, but the Indian National Congress, led by Mahatma Gandhi, refused.

Gandhi believed that India should not support a war being waged by colonisers who had oppressed the Indian people for more than 200 years. He also believed that the war would benefit the British at the expense of the Indians. Instead, he proposed that India demand independence from Britain as a condition for joining the war.

About Mahadev Desai

Mahatma Gandhi's personal secretary, Mahadev Desai, died on 15th August, 1942, while imprisoned in Aga Khan Palace during the Quit India Movement. He died at the age of 59 after contracting a severe case of pneumonia. Gandhi was deeply affected by his death, which he described as an "irreparable loss".

Mahatma Gandhi and Mahadev Desai

However, the British government rejected Gandhi's proposal. On 9th August, in 1942, Gandhi was arrested and taken to Poona. There, he was detained in Aga Khan Palace, along with his wife, Kasturba, his secretary, Mahadev Desai, and other leaders, such as Sarojini Naidu and Pyarelal Nayyar. The leaders of the Working Committee, including Maulana Azad, Sardar Vallabhbhai Patel, and Jawaharlal Nehru, were held in the Fort in Ahmednagar.

The same month, the Congress Party launched the Quit India Movement, calling for the immediate withdrawal of British Colonial rule from India. On September 9, 1942 Gandhi made a speech from Gowalia Tank Maidan in Bombay; conveying the message of Do or Die to the Indian masses. The movement called for widespread civil disobedience, involving strikes, protests, and nonviolent resistance to British rule.

Soulmates for Life
Kasturba Gandhi's health had been declining since 1943. Despite attempts to treat her illness, she passed away in February 1944 with Gandhi by her side. Just days before her death, she told Gandhi, "Now I am going." The couple had a unique bond forged over 60 years of shared struggles, self-discovery, and pursuit of truth, and nonviolence.

Efforts were made to disrupt communication and transportation in India, with fish plates and rails being removed, bridges being blown up, and telegraph wires being cut. Students and young people were heavily involved in the protests, which forced schools and colleges to remain closed for months. Many protesters were shot while carrying the national flag, and there were widespread arrests and detentions without charge. Unarmed crowds were attacked with machine guns and air strikes.

India Achieves Independence

After being released from prison in 1944, Gandhi hoped to negotiate with the British to gain independence for India. However, Muhammad Ali Jinnah intensified his demanded for a separate country for Muslims. In September 1944, Gandhi and Jinnah exchanged many letters and met several times to discuss India's future. Gandhi desired a united and independent India in which all religions could coexist, but Jinnah disagreed and advocated for a separate Muslim state, which became Pakistan. This led to widespread tension and conflict between the Hindu and Muslim communities across India.

As India's political situation grew worse, the Quit India movement lost momentum. Meanwhile, the British government was battling violence and protests. They eventually agreed to divide India and form two separate countries: India and Pakistan.

This decision led to one of the largest mass migrations in human history, displacing millions and killing hundreds of thousands in the ensuing violence. The partition and the violence it sparked deeply troubled Gandhi. He fasted in the hopes of promoting peace and harmony between the two communities. His efforts were partially successful, as violence decreased in some areas.

India and Pakistan finally gained their independence in 1947, with Jawaharlal Nehru becoming India's first prime minister and Muhammad Ali Jinnah Pakistan's founder and governor-general. On 15th August, 1947, the day of India's independence from British rule, Gandhi did not engage in any celebratory activities. Instead, he fasted and spun cotton, in Calcutta, as a means of promoting peace and unity among the people of India.

Legacy

On the ill-fated evening of 30th January, 1948, at around 5.17 pm, Gandhi was strolling in the garden of Birla House (now known as Gandhi Smriti), in Delhi, in the company of his grandnieces. Sardar Vallabhbhai Patel had come to meet him and Gandhi was conversing with him. He hated being late, especially for prayers. So, when he realised it was getting late, he took leave and quickly walked to the prayer ground.

When he got close to the raised ground, a man approached and tried to touch Gandhi's feet. Suddenly, he bowed down and fired three bullets at the Mahatma from a concealed pistol at point blank range. The assailant was Nathuram Godse, a Hindu nationalist. Accounts of Gandhi's demise vary: some believe that he perished immediately, while others maintain that he was taken to a bedroom in Birla House and breathed his last as a relative read verses from Hindu texts.

Gandhi Smriti at Birla House, New Delhi

On the evening of 30th January, just hours after Gandhi's demise, India's first Prime Minister, Jawaharlal Nehru, delivered a famous speech on All India Radio (AIR), saying:

"Friends and comrades, the light has gone out of our lives, and there is darkness everywhere, and I do not quite know what to tell you or how to say it. Our beloved leader, Bapu as we called him, the father of the nation, is no more. Perhaps I am wrong to say that; nevertheless, we will not see him again, as we have seen him for these many years, we will not run to him for advice or seek solace from him, and that is a terrible blow, not only for me, but for millions and millions in this country."

Despite the shock and grief, Nehru urged the people to remain calm and carry on with their lives in a peaceful manner. He also urged them to continue working for a free and united India based on nonviolence and equality in order to honour Gandhi's legacy.

India descended into chaos and mourning. Many public events were cancelled after the government declared a state of emergency. People took to the streets to express their grief and anger over his death. An 8-km-long funeral procession was carried out from Birla House to Raj Ghat, the memorial site, and was attended by more than a million people. Scores of people thronged the side lines as the funeral procession made its way to Raj Ghat – it took almost five hours for the procession to reach the site.

Place where cremation of Mahatma Gandhi took place - Rajghat, New Delhi

The chassis of a weapons carrier was taken apart overnight to fix a high-floor to transport Gandhi's body and so that people could see him as they passed by. The vehicle's engine was left unused; instead, it took a team of 50 individuals each holding onto one of four drag-ropes to pull the vehicle forward.

As per Hindu tradition, Gandhi's body was cremated and his ashes were stored in urns. The urns were then taken to different parts of India for memorial services. On 12th February, 1948, most of the ashes were immersed at the Sangam in Allahabad. In 1997, Tushar Gandhi, Gandhi's great-grandson, found an urn with Gandhi's ashes in a bank vault and reclaimed it legally. He scattered the ashes at the Sangam too. Some of Gandhi's ashes were also immersed in the River Nile near Jinja, Uganda, and a memorial plaque now stands to commemorate the event. An urn was placed at the Aga Khan Palace in Pune, where Gandhi was detained from 1942 to 1944. Lastly, an urn was placed at the Self Realization Fellowship Lake Shrine in Los Angeles, United States.

Reactions

After the assassination of Gandhi, there was a tremendous outpouring of support and condolences from leaders across the world. Many expressed their shock and sadness at the news of his death. Leaders from different countries spoke out about the importance of nonviolence and the legacy that Gandhi left behind. There were calls for justice and peace, as well as mourning for the loss of such an important figure. Here are some of the tributes that were paid by leaders in India as well as overseas to the Father of the Nation:

C. Rajagopalachari, the last Governor-General of India, expressed his grief, saying, "No one could die a more glorious death than Mahatma Gandhi. He was going to the seat of his prayer to speak to his Rama. He did not die in the bed calling for hot water, doctors or nurses. He did not die after mumbling incoherent words in the sick bed. He died standing, not even sitting down, Rama was too eager to take him even before he could reach the seat of his prayer."

Sardar Vallabhbhai Patel, the former Deputy Prime Minister of India and Gandhi's long-time associate, observed that Gandhi had made a huge sacrifice – one that would "wake up the conscience of our nation countrymen and evoke a higher response in the heart of every Indian." He called upon the citizens of the country, asking the citizens of the country to "… stand united and bravely face the national disaster that has overtaken us." He also asked the people to "solemnly pledge … to Gandhiji's teachings and ideals."

Notable political activist and poet, Sarojini Naidu, expressed her feelings in poignant words, saying "Mahatma Gandhi, whose frail body was committed to the flames yesterday, is not dead. It was right that the cremation took place in the midst of the dead kings who were buried in Delhi, for he was the kingliest of all kings…. Far greater than all the warriors who led the armies to battle was this little man, the bravest, the most tried friend of all. Delhi has become the centre and sanctuary of the great revolutionary who emancipated his enslave country from foreign bondage and gave it to its freedom and its flag."

Maulana Abdul Kalam Azad, the former Education Minister of India, remarked that Gandhi had "carried on his frail shoulders a great deal of burden of humanity and now it was for them to stand together and share it." He concluded that "(if) millions of Indians could divide that burden and carry it successfully, it would be nothing short of a miracle."

Lord Mountbatten, the last Viceroy of British India, highlighted that Gandhi led a life based on the ideals of love and truth. He observed that Gandhi's demise was "a loss to mankind which sorely needs the living light of those ideals of love and tolerance for which he strove and died." Reflecting on Gandhi's "life of truth, tolerance and love towards his fellows," he hoped that it would inspire the people of the world to follow in his footsteps.

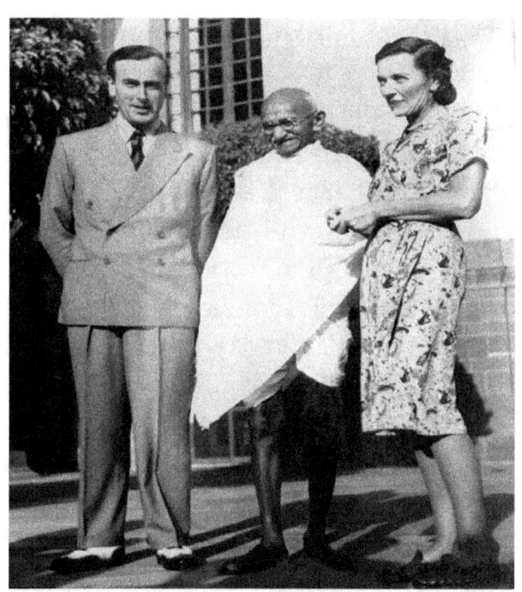

Mahatma Gandhi with Lord and Lady Mountbatten

President Harry S. Truman of the United States observed, "... (Gandhi's) teachings and actions have left a deep impression on millions of people. As a teacher and leader, his influence made itself felt not only in India, but everywhere in the world and his death brings great sorrow to all peace loving people.... I know that the people of Asia will be inspired by his tragic death to strive with increased determination to achieve the goals of cooperation and mutual trust for which the Mahatma has now given his life."

Muhammad Ali Jinnah, the Founder and first Governor-General of Pakistan, said that he associated with all the tributes that had been paid to Gandhi. He further added that Gandhi had died while discharging his duty – a noble thought in which he believed. "His tragic death, however much we may deplore it and however much we may condemn the murderer, was a noble death, for he died in the discharge of his duty," Jinnah reflected.

His Holiness Pope Pius XII, former Head of the Catholic Church in Vatican City, noted that Gandhi was "the spiritual leader of millions of Indians and had always struggled for peace."

In the same vein, HH The Dalai Lama, stated, "His life has inspired me ever since I was a small boy. *Ahimsa* or nonviolence is the powerful idea that Mahatma Gandhi made familiar throughout the world. ... As Mahatma Gandhi showed by his own example, nonviolence can be implemented not only in politics but also in day-to-day life. ... He showed that nonviolence should be active in helping others. ... If we can actively do this I believe we will be fulfilling Mahatma Gandhi's legacy to us. It is my prayer that, as we enter this new century, nonviolence and dialogue will increasingly come to govern all human relations."

Famous physicist Albert Einstein said, "... He died as the victim of his own principles, the principle of nonviolence. He died because in time of disorder and general irritation in his country, he refused armed protection for himself. It was his unshakable belief that the use of force is an evil in itself, that therefore it must be avoided by those who are striving for supreme justice to his belief. ..."

Gandhi's legacy continues to inspire scores of people across the world who strive to live their life by his timeless ideals of love, compassion, peace, nonviolence, and truth.

Teachings and Philosophy

To say Gandhi led an extremely enriching life is an understatement. His letters, lectures, statements, and books have piqued the interest of global thinkers, philosophers, and scholars. It's also worth noting that different thinkers and scholars have different perspectives on his life. While some have described Gandhi as the embodiment of truth, love, and compassion, others have emphasised his complex, multi-layered, and frequently contradictory personality, as a result of the changing course of events around him.

Gandhi's childhood, considering that he was raised in a Hindu and Jain household in his native Gujarat, had a significant impact on his beliefs. His mother, a devoted Vaishnava, was one of the major influences on his early thoughts about life. Gandhi spent a lot of time meditating on other religions and ideologies, including Islam, Christianity, Buddhism, and Advaita Vedanta, as well as Bhakti saint literature from India. Other authors and thinkers who had an impact on him included Tolstoy and Thoreau.

Gandhi as an Advaitist Hindu

Mahatma Gandhi declared himself to be an Advaitist Hindu at the age of 57. However, he also supported Dvaitist viewpoints and religious pluralism.

The events that occurred after Gandhi moved to South Africa shaped the core concepts of his philosophy. According to famous political theorist Bhikhu Parekh, Gandhi's ideas in South Africa were influenced by the books *On the Duty of Civil Disobedience* by Henry David Thoreau, *Ethical Religion* by William Salter, and *The Kingdom of God is Within You* by Leo Tolstoy.

In fact, Tolstoy wrote *A Letter to a Hindu* that focused on the idea of embodying love as a weapon of passive resistance to help Indians overthrow the British Colonial rule. Gandhi asked Tolstoy's permission to republish the piece in Gujarati in 1919. Both went on to correspond via letters over the years, discussing the concept of nonviolence as well as their opposition to colonialism and state authority.

Another person who served as an early influence in Gandhi's life was Shrimad Rajchandra, who was a notable Jain philosopher and poet. Gandhi went on to keep in touch with him even when he moved to South Africa. In 1930, he wrote "I have said elsewhere that in moulding my inner life Tolstoy and Ruskin vied with Kavi (as he lovingly referred to Rajchandra). But Kavi's influence was undoubtedly deeper if only because I had come in closest personal touch with him."

Gandhi's Thoughts on Truth and Nonviolence

Truth was not just a concept or an idea for Mahatma Gandhi – it was a way of life. He believed in Absolute Truth, which he believed could only be attained through introspection and self-reflection. According to him, the biggest battle that a person had to face in their lifetime was to overcome one's own fears and insecurities. This is manifested in his statement, "God is Truth", which he later changed to "Truth is God".

He also believed in the power of truth and its ability to triumph over all odds. Gandhi saw truth as the ultimate weapon in the fight against oppression and injustice. He dedicated his life to spreading it through nonviolent means.

Perhaps the most well-known of Gandhi's nonviolent philosophies was that of *satyagraha*, which means "holding on to the truth". He believed that *satyagraha* was a way for people to fight for their rights while maintaining their dignity and humanity.

Gandhi grounded the principle of *satyagraha* on the Vedantic ideas of universal love, self-realisation, nonviolence, and vegetarianism. He used this technique in several movements he launched in India, including the Salt March and the Quit India Movement, to fight British Colonial rule.

According to Gandhi, *satyagraha* was a way for people to transform themselves and society at large. It demanded a deep commitment to truth and nonviolence, as well as accepting responsibility for one's actions. Gandhi hoped to build a society based on justice, equality, and compassion by using *satyagraha* as the means to achieve independence.

As an extension of the philosophy of *satyagraha*, he launched the civil disobedience and non-cooperation movement, which was based on his idea that "the endurance of suffering is a means to an end". In this perspective, the "end" was to lead to the upliftment of society at large.

The Philosophy of Nonviolence

The principle of nonviolence has long been preached across religion and spirituality. Since time immemorial, nonviolence has been seen as a highly regarded virtue. However, Gandhi was the first to apply it as one of the aspects of his political strategy. He wrote about it extensively in his autobiography, *The Story of My Experiments with Truth*.

Gandhi was a great leader and philosopher who practised nonviolence in his daily life. He believed that violence breeds more violence and that peaceful solutions are always preferable to the use of force. Gandhi's ideas of nonviolence, also known as *ahimsa*, were influenced by his religious beliefs, particularly Jainism and Hinduism.

Nonviolence was a moral and spiritual principle for Gandhi, not just a political strategy. He believed that we should never harm others through thought, word, or deed, and that we should always seek peaceful resolutions to conflicts. He also believed that nonviolence required a great deal of courage and strength of character because it required standing up for what was right without resorting to violence.

Gandhi's ideas of nonviolence had an impact across the world, inspiring civil rights leaders, such as Martin Luther King Jr. and Nelson Mandela. His message of nonviolent resistance continues to inspire people all over the world even today who seek justice and equality.

The Concept of Swaraj or Self-rule

The concept of *swaraj*, or self-rule, was central to Gandhi's philosophy of nonviolence and civil disobedience. He believed that Indians had the right to self-government and should not be subject to the rule of a foreign power. Gandhi's concept of *swaraj* included not only political, but also spiritual and economic freedom.

Gandhi saw the struggle for *swaraj* as a way to transform Indian society and achieve greater social and economic equality. He urged people to take charge of their own lives and work towards the creation of a just and equitable society. He envisioned a society founded on the values of truth, nonviolence, and self-sufficiency. He believed that true *swaraj* could be attained only when individuals accepted responsibility for their own lives and worked for the greater good.

Gandhi's ideas on *swaraj* had a long-lasting impact on Indian politics and society. His emphasis on self-government and nonviolence continues to inspire people all over the world who are fighting for liberty and social justice.

Nonviolence and Vegetarianism

Gandhi was born into a Modh *baniya* family and raised as a vegetarian. Vegetarianism was central to Hindu Vaishnavite and Jain traditions in his native Gujarat. As a result, eating meat was seen a method of inflicting violence on animals. According to Gandhi, most forms of food required some form of harm to a living organism. However, he believed that one could aim to understand these interrelationships and reduce the extent to which such violence is inflicted on them.

Gandhi and Animal Rights

Mahatma Gandhi opposed animal cruelty. He campaigned against dissection and vivisection for medical studies. He believed it caused pain and suffering and considered it a form of violence against animals.

As a result, Gandhi focused on finding food sources that would cause as little harm to animals as possible. To him, food was only a necessity for survival, and there was a need to consider how it might affect other living organisms. Gandhi abstained from not only meat, but also milk and eggs. The *Moral Basis of Vegetarianism* is one of his most famous works on vegetarianism. He also contributed to the publication of the London Vegetarian Society.

8

Notable Achievements

Mahatma Gandhi is well-known for his numerous accomplishments that made an impact not just on the lives of people in India, but across the world. He is widely admired for his principles of nonviolence and civil disobedience, which inspired many social and political movements around the world. He is frequently cited as an inspiration for leaders, such as Martin Luther King Jr. and Nelson Mandela, both of whom employed his principles to initiate social change.

In addition, Gandhi's philosophy of self-reliance and self-sufficiency went on to make a long-term impact on India's economic development. He believed that small-scale industries and the promotion of traditional crafts and skills could help India achieve economic independence.

Finally, the achievements of Mahatma Gandhi have left an indelible mark on the world. His thoughts, ideas, principles, and teachings pertaining to nonviolence, civil disobedience, and self-reliance continue to inspire people around the world and serve as a reminder that change through peaceful means is possible. Here is a snapshot of Gandhi's notable achievements through the years:

1. Gandhi's nonviolent civil disobedience campaigns against the British played a vital role in securing India's independence in 1947.

2. Despite being nominated five times, Gandhi was never awarded the Nobel Peace Prize. However, after his assassination, the Nobel Committee recognised his contributions and awarded him a posthumous Special Commemorative Award in 1948.

3. In 1931, *Time Magazine* named Gandhi "Person of the Year," recognising his leadership and contributions to the Indian independence movement.

4. A strong advocate of women's rights, Gandhi encouraged women to participate in the Indian independence movement. He advocated for equal rights for men and women and promoted education for girls. Gandhi also spoke up against child marriage and the dowry system.

5. Gandhi believed in the ideals of self-reliance and self-sufficiency. He applied this to the development of rural areas because he believed in empowering villages by promoting cottage industries, small-scale businesses, and agriculture. He also stood for using traditional methods of production to promote local industries.

6. His philosophy of nonviolence inspired many civil rights movements around the world, including the US civil rights movement led by Martin Luther King Jr.

7. The Salt March was a significant event in India's independence movement, in which Gandhi led a 386-km march to the Arabian Sea to protest the British salt tax.

8. His Khadi Movement encouraged Indians to spin and weave their clothing as a way to work towards creating economic independence.

9. Gandhi vehemently criticised the practice of untouchability and worked to remove the social stigma associated with it.

10. Gandhi believed that the development of agriculture was crucial for India's economic growth. He advocated the use of organic farming methods and encouraged farmers

to use natural resources instead of chemical fertilizers and pesticides.

11. Gandhi also worked to reform India's prisons, promoting education and training programs for inmates, and recommended better living conditions for them.

12. Gandhi worked tirelessly to promote unity between Hindus and Muslims in India, advocating for equal rights for both communities.

13. Posthumously awarded the Templeton Prize for Religious Progress in 2002, Mahatma Gandhi was recognised for his contributions to the promotion of religious harmony and understanding.

14. The United Nations designated 2nd October, which is Gandhi's birthday, as the International Day of Nonviolence in 2007, to honour his nonviolent philosophy and its contributions to world peace.

(a) Gandhi focused on constructive activities in villages during the intervening years between Non-cooperation and Civil Disobedience Movement

(b) In the quest of achieving self-reliance, Gandhi popularised usage Charkha and Khadi cloth

(c) Gandhi propogated importance of Nai Talim which focused on Learning by Doing

9

Mahatma Gandhi's Famous Quotes

Here are a few inspiring quotes by Mahatma Gandhi that continue to inspire people to live up to their highest potential across the world:

- "Be the change that you wish to see in the world."
- "An eye for an eye will only make the whole world blind."
- "The weak can never forgive. Forgiveness is the attribute of the strong."
- "Freedom is not worth having if it does not include the freedom to make mistakes."
- "The best way to find yourself is to lose yourself in the service of others."
- "A man is but the product of his thoughts. What he thinks, he becomes."
- "It is unwise to be too sure of one's own wisdom. It is healthy to be reminded that the strongest might weaken and the wisest might err."
- "There are people in the world so hungry, that God cannot appear to them except in the form of bread."
- "You must not lose faith in humanity. Humanity is like an ocean; if a few drops of the ocean are dirty, the ocean does not become dirty."

- "Happiness is when what you think, what you say, and what you do are in harmony."
- "The weak can never forgive. Forgiveness is the attribute of the strong."
- "My religion is based on truth and nonviolence. Truth is my God. Nonviolence is the means of realising Him."
- "All the religions of the world, while they may differ in other respects, unitedly proclaim that nothing lives in this world but Truth."
- "The greatness of humanity is not in being human, but in being humane."

Learning from Gandhi's Life

Mahatma Gandhi once said, "When I am dead and buried, I will speak from my grave." Even though it has been more than 80 years since Gandhi's demise, his words continue to resonate in the world as a philosophy of love, hope, and compassion for humanity. Gandhi was a man of extraordinary integrity, compassion, and conviction. He was a strong advocate for nonviolence and civil disobedience, and his legacy continues to inspire people all over the world.

The power of peaceful resistance is perhaps the most important lesson we can take from Gandhi's life. Gandhi maintained his commitment to nonviolence throughout his life, even in the face of intense opposition and persecution. He demonstrated that change can be achieved without the use of violence or aggression, and that true strength comes from standing up for what you believe in, irrespective of the cost.

Another important lesson from Gandhi's life is the value of leading by example. Gandhi did not simply preach his beliefs – he lived them every day and his actions inspired others to do the same. Gandhi was a role model for those around him, whether he was leading peaceful protests, fasting for political change, or simply living a simple and humble life.

Gandhi's life teaches us the value of perseverance and determination. His teachings are yet to be embodied by the

Indian populace at large and his principles are yet to be employed for resolving issues related to poverty, unemployment, and communalism. That said, scores of activists and civil society institutions have been embodying his philosophy to fight for the upliftment of the underprivileged.

Even though we still have a long way to go in our fight for peace and prosperity for all sections of society, we must take a leaf out of Gandhi's outlook towards making persistent efforts and never giving up in the face of struggle. Throughout his life, Gandhi faced numerous challenges and setbacks, but he always stood by his principles or goals. He remained dedicated to his cause until the end, and his legacy inspires us all to strive for a better world.